I ask only to be free. The butterflies are free." So said the deceitful Mr. Skimpole in the presence of one of his creditors, in Charles Dickens's *Bleak House*.

It is difficult to escape the illusion that butterflies lead a carefree existence, as we watch them peacefully visiting flowers or fluttering over a meadow. But we all know that butterflies are not really free. They are as bound by their instincts as we are by social conventions and by instincts of our own. Their apparently simple lives are actually quite demanding. A butterfly's survival and that of its offspring depend on finding enough food; on the right choice of a time and place to lay eggs; on correctly performing the intricate rituals of courtship; on picking the best time and place to lay eggs; on finding a safe spot to spend the quiet time during the transformation from larva

Top to bottom: Pipevine Swallowtail *(Battus philenor)*, North America. Tiger Swallowtail, *(Pterourus glaucus)*, dark form, eastern North America.

Above: **Spicebush Swallowtail** *(Pterourus troilus)*, **eastern North America.** *Below:* **Giant Swallowtail** *(Heraclides cresphontes),* **eastern North America.**

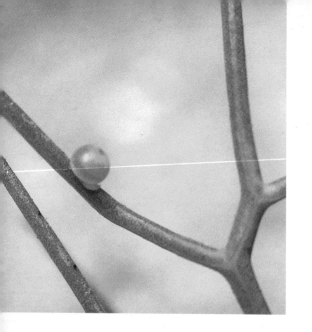

to adult; on the right behavior for avoiding predators, bad weather, and the hazards of nighttime; and, for some, on defending a territory or on beginning a migration at the right time and traveling to the right place. The price of a single wrong choice is a high one.

Anise Swallowtail *(Papilio zelicaon)*, western North America. This species lays its egg (top left) mainly on the native Sweet Fennel and also on Queen Anne's Lace and other members of the parsley family. The young larva (top right), feeds on tender leaves and flower buds and is banded with black, orange, and white; at maturity (center), it is 2 inches long, and mainly green to match the color of the plant. The chrysalis (bottom) is attached to a twig by a fine silken girdle.

The newly emerged butterfly (right) hangs from the empty chrysalis until its folded wings expand. The adult (bottom) visits a variety of flowers, including Poison Hemlock, one of the larval food plants.

Apollo *(Parnassius apollo)*, **Europe, western Asia.**

In meeting these challenges, butterflies are aided not only by their ancient, inherited behavior patterns but also by the way they are built. As with other insects, the compact bodies of adults are divided into three parts: the head, which includes the antennae or "feelers," the eyes, and the mouth; the thorax, which bears six legs and two pairs of wings, and contains the muscles that move them; and the abdomen or "tail," which contains most internal organs. Unlike ours, their skeleton is on the outside – a tough, waterproof coating that protects the delicate structures inside and provides support for muscles. Although moths are related to butterflies, they are mainly nocturnal, and have knobbed rather than feathery or threadlike antennae.

Top to bottom: **Brimstone (*Gonepteryx rhamni*), Eurasia, North Africa. Common Sulphur (*Colias philodice*), North America. Orange Sulphur (*Colias eurytheme*), North America.**

Butterflies and moths belong to the group Lepidoptera, meaning "scale-wings." The four wings of butterflies – their most conspicuous feature – are coated with thousands of tiny pigmented scales; most of the bright colors of butterflies, as well as the soft tints and patterns that offer camouflage, are produced by these pigments. In many species, the uppersides of the wings are brightly colored but the undersides are camouflaged; a butterfly like the Question Mark only needs to close its wings over its back to escape detection. The purple and blue in the wings of many species, including those conveniently called "blues," is produced not by pigments but by light reflected from microscopic prisms in the scales. A few butterflies, mostly tropical species like *Haetera piera*, have large areas without scales. These transparent patches make such butterflies harder to see in the dim forest interior, and are a form of camouflage.

This page: Orange Tip *(Anthocharis cardamines)*, Eurasia. *Opposite:* Large White *(Pieris brassicae)*, Eurasia, North Africa.

These colors and patterns enable butterflies, as well as butterfly-watchers, to recognize the different species, but the colors of some species also serve other functions. In the Monarch, the Pipevine Swallowtail, and the longwings of tropical America, bold patterns and colors serve as a warning that the butterflies, whose caterpillars have fed on poisonous plants, are poisonous themselves. This warning is so effective in discouraging predators that certain non-poisonous species mimic the toxic ones, thus gaining protection from enemies who can see the similarity but not the difference.

Opposite: Monarch *(Danaus plexippus),* North America. Top, larva; below, adult. *This page, clockwise:* Grayling *(Hipparchia semele),* Europe. Queen *(Danaus gilippus),* southern United States to South America. Little Wood Satyr *(Megisto cymela),* eastern North America. Marbled White *(Melanargia galathea),* Europe, western Asia, North Africa.

Opposite: Gatekeeper *(Pyronia tithonus)*, Europe, western Asia. *Above:* Large Wood Nymph *(Cercyonis pegala)*, North America. *Below:* Julia *(Dryas iulia)*, southern United States to South America.

Great Spangled Fritillary *(Speyeria cybele)*, **North America.**

The Monarch is mimicked by the Viceroy; the Pipevine Swallowtail is imitated by several dark swallowtails and by the Red-spotted Purple; and a whole host of species mimic the tropical longwings.

The wings of some butterflies are equipped with features that provide protection in different ways. In the Buckeye of North America, the Peacock Butterfly of Eurasia, and many others, round spots that resemble eyes, draw the attention of an attacking predator. The predator, usually a bird, goes for the conspicuous target; the butterfly escapes, minus its eyespot, but still able to fly perfectly well. Survivors of such attacks can often be identified by a beak-shaped gap in the margin of one of their wings. In the hairstreaks, the hind wings bear slender filaments that resemble antennae and may even be moved, causing predators to mistake the butterfly's back end for its front. When the attack comes, the butterfly is able to escape by flying away in the "wrong" direction.

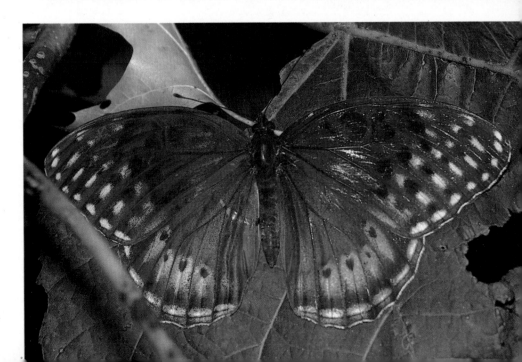

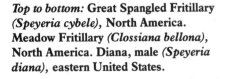

Top to bottom: **Great Spangled Fritillary** *(Speyeria cybele)*, North America. **Meadow Fritillary** *(Clossiana bellona)*, North America. **Diana, male** *(Speyeria diana)*, eastern United States.

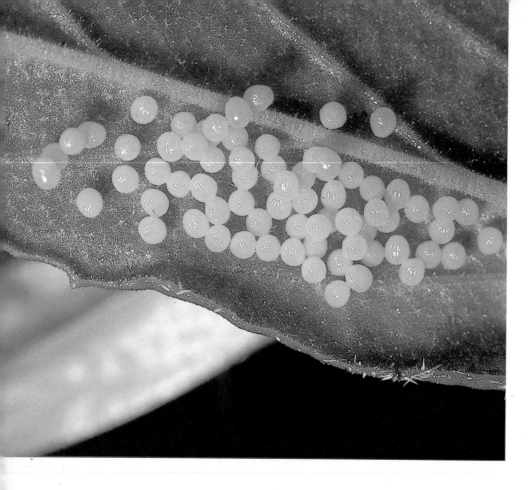

Most insects have simple jaws that move from side to side rather than up and down like ours. The mouthparts of adult butterflies, with their diet of liquid nectar, are modified into a coiled tube like a drinking straw. While a majority of butterflies visit flowers and sip nectar, many species use their drinking straws to obtain other kinds of nutritious liquids. Mourning Cloaks drink fermented sap from wounded or dying trees, while other butterflies sip at mineral-rich water from mud puddles, the fluids of decaying animal carcasses, and even the urine of animals that have gathered at muddy waterholes.

Like most insects, butterflies have a life cycle that includes four stages: the egg; the larva in butterflies called a caterpillar; the pupa, a resting stage in which the caterpillar quietly changes into an adult; and the adult. The adult seeks food only for energy and not for growth, and usually lives but a short time.

Chalcedon Checkerspot *(Occidryas chalcedona),* **western North America. Like other checkerspots, the Chalcedon lays its eggs in clusters (above) on a variety of plants, including plantains and honeysuckles. Newly hatched larvae (below) first eat the shell of their own eggs, and then turn to the leaves of their food plant.**

The first task of an adult, aside from staying alive, is to find a mate. In many species, males emerge before females, and are waiting when the females reach the end of their pupal stage. In others, among them the Red Admiral, males set up territories, attacking all trespassers except a female of their own species. In still others, males congregate in special places and females visit these sites for mating. Male swallowtails often "hilltop," gathering on the top of a hill to await the arrival of females.

Chalcedon Checkerspot *(Occidryas chalcedona)*, western North America. Older larvae (above) bearing many spines, feed in groups, usually in a flimsy nest of silk. The chrysalis (below) lasts all winter, attached by its tail end to the underside of a leaf; by spring, the markings of the wings can be seen along its sides.

Opposite: Chalcedon Checkerspot
(Occidryas chalcedona), western North
America. *Above:* Baltimore *(Euphydryas
phaeton),* eastern North America. *Right:*
Pearly Crescentspot *(Phyciodes tharos),*
North America.

This page: **Question Mark *(Polygonia interrogationis)*, eastern North America.**

Butterflies recognize a potential mate first by sight and then by special odors. Mating is preceded by a number of special postures and rituals; each part of the ceremony must be performed in the right way and at the right moment, or the spell is broken. Once mating is accomplished, the sexes separate – the males to seek another mate, the females to begin the all-important task of finding a place to lay eggs.

The eggs of butterflies are often spherical, as with the Anise Swallowtail and the Chalcedon Checkerspot. Other shapes include the ribbed lemon of the Monarch, the spindles of the sulphurs and whites, and the squat turbans of the coppers and hairstreaks. While many species lay their eggs singly, with the female depositing them on the undersides of young, tender leaves or in clusters of flower buds, some, including the Chalcedon Checkerspot and Mourning Cloak, do lay their eggs in groups.

Female butterflies must take care to lay their eggs in the right plant, for while the adults can take food from many different flowers and other sources, caterpillars are particular about what plants they will eat. Females recognize the right plant by "tasting" it with sense organs on their hind legs. The caterpillars of the Monarch can only eat the

foliage of the poisonous milk-
weeds and dogbanes, while
those of the Viceroy prefer
willows but also eat the leaves
of aspens, apples, and cherries.
Larvae of the Orange Tip of
Eurasia must have the foliage of
certain relatives of the mustards.
Those of the American Painted
Lady feed only on everlastings
and a few related plants. Caterpillars of the Snout Butterfly

This page: **Buckeye (*Junonoa coenia*),
North America. *Overleaf:* Peacock
Butterfly (*Inachis io*), Eurasia.**

and Hackberry Butterfly will only accept the leaves of hackberries; the two species are not found in places where these trees are absent.

Caterpillars are shaped like worms, but have a well-defined head, with eyes, and six pairs of legs as do the adults. To further assist them in creeping about on their food plants, they have five pairs of false legs, or "prolegs," on the hind end, which correspond to the abdomen in the adult. Unlike adults, caterpillars have strong jaws for chewing foliage. They have been described as "eating machines," and indeed the only things a caterpillar has to do is eat, grow, and avoid predators. A few prey on aphids, and a few of the blues live in ants' nests, where they are tended by the ants and return this kindness by eating the eggs and larvae of their hosts. But nearly all caterpillars are strict vegetarians, and some, such as those of the Giant Swallowtail, which eats the foliage of citrus trees, are even considered agricultural pests.

Top and center: **American Painted Lady** *(Vanessa virginiensis),* **North America.** *Bottom:* **Red Admiral** *(Vanessa atlanta),* **North America, Eurasia.** *Opposite:* **Small Tortoiseshell** *(Aglais urticae),* **Eurasia.**

Most caterpillars are secretive and protectively colored, often in green. The larvae of fritillaries, which eat violets, are nocturnal and almost impossible to find during the day. Those of the Giant Swallowtail mimic bird droppings when they are small, and when they are older, they have orange, foul-smelling "scent horns" that discourage predators. Many caterpillars wear spines or hairs that keep parasitic wasps from injecting their eggs into the caterpillar's body. The caterpillars of toxic species like the Monarch are as boldly patterned as the adults, giving a warning signal like that of their winged parents. The larvae of the longwings, also toxic, wear both spines and bold colors.

Since a caterpillar's skeleton is on the outside of the body, it must shed it skin as it grows. The appearance of a caterpillar may change with each molt, and the stage between two molts is known as an instar. Depending on the species, there are from four to six instars before the caterpillar reaches full size.

Opposite: **Red-spotted Purple** *(Limenitis astyanax)*, North America. *This page:* **White Admiral** *(Limenitis arthemis)*, **North America. Mourning Cloak** *(Nymphalis antiopa)*, **Eurasia, North America to northern South America. Poplar Admiral** *(Limenitis populi)*, **Eurasia.**

When it finally reaches maturity, it undergoes a molt in which its appearance changes profoundly. Before this important molt the caterpillar stops eating and searches out a safe spot; it may find a hiding place on the food-plant or leave its foodplant and hide among dry leaves on the ground. Although it still looks like a caterpillar on the outside, a dramatic reorganization has already begun on the inside.

This page and opposite: **Purple Emperor (Apatura iris),** Eurasia.

Hackberry Butterfly *(Asterocampa celtis),* eastern North America.

When the last larval covering is shed, what is revealed is a sculptured and camouflaged capsule. This is the pupa, the resting stage that precedes the emergence of the adult. Although the pupae of many moths wear a protective cocoon of silk, among butterflies only the skippers spin such a silken cocoon. The exposed pupa of a butterfly is called a chrysalis, and may hang down from the underside of a leaf or stem, as in the Monarch and Chalcedon Checkerspot, or rest against a stem or other object, supported by a silken girdle, as in the Anise Swallowtail, other swallowtails, and the sulphurs and whites. In some species, such as the hairstreaks, the chrysalis is simply attached to a support of some kind, and in the skippers, the pupa lies in the ground, usually protected by a cocoon.

Inside, the reorganization continues, and as the emergence of the adult draws near, its colorful wings can be seen through the thin wall of the chrysalis. Finally the appointed day arrives.

Snout Butterfly *(Libytheana bachmanii)*, eastern North America. Red-bordered Metalmark *(Caria ino)*, southern Texas and Mexico. Viceroy *(Limenitis archippus)*, North America.

Above: Coral Hairstreak *(Harkenclenus
titus)*, North America. *Left:* Great Purple
Hairstreak *(tlides halesus)*, North America.

Usually at night or in the damp, quiet hours near dawn, the chrysalis splits open, and the adult, its wings still folded and crumpled, climbs out. The new butterfly hangs motionless – as if dazed – for several hours, its wings gradually expanding to full size. This is perhaps the most perilous time for a butterfly. It is completely defenseless, and if there is insufficient dampness, the wings may dry and harden before they are fully expanded, leaving the insect permanently crippled. Because of this need for dampness, the best time to look for new adults is the day after a rainstorm. If all goes well, an adult butterfly soon flies off to begin the cycle once again.

The time span of a complete life cycle varies greatly. The Spring Azure and southern populations of the American Copper have several generations or "broods" a year. There tend to be fewer broods per year in colder climates than in warmer ones, and fewer in Europe than in North America. For species with several broods a season, the length of a single cycle can

be measured in months or even weeks. But in many species there is only one brood a year, and in this case the cycle is a long one in which the winter may be spent in any of the four stages. The most common stages for riding out the winter are eggs and pupae, since these are stages that need not eat. But in some species, among them the Mourning Cloak, Question Mark, and the Brimstone of Eurasia and North Africa, the adult is the stage that winter's over. On a warm day in winter, any of these species may emerge from hibernation and fly about briefly.

Opposite: American (or Small) Copper *(Lycaena phlaeas)*, North America, Eurasia. Bronze Copper *(Hyllolycaena hyllus)*, North America. *This page:* Eastern Tailed Blue *(Everes comyntas)*, North America, Central America. *Right:* Spring Azure *(Celastrina ladon)*, North America, Central America.

Opposite: Common Blue *(Polyommatus icarus)*, Eurasia, North Africa. Adonis Blue *(Lysandra bellargus)*, Europe, southwestern Asia. *This page, clockwise:* Duke of Burgundy Fritillary *(Hamearis lucina)*, Europe. Least Skipper *(Ancyloxypha numitor)*, eastern North America. Green-backed Skipper *(Perichares philetes)*, southern Texas to Argentina. Silver-spotted Skipper *(Epargyreus clarus)*, North America.

Preceding pages: **Peacock Pansy** *(Precis almana),* **Southeast Asia.** *This page:* **(Precis orithya), Southeast Asia.** *Left:* **(Delias), Southeast Asia.**

Blue Crow *(Euploea mulciber)*, Southeast Asia. *Right:* Birdwing *(Ornithoptera)*, Indonesia.

In a few butterflies, the last adults to emerge before winter do not hibernate, but instead travel south to avoid the cold. The most famous of these is the Monarch, which migrates thousands of miles each fall to winter in California and Mexico. The wintering places in Mexico contain millions of insects, representing nearly all parts of the vast breeding range of this widespread North American butterfly. Other sites are tourist attractions along the coast of California. When spring arrives, the Monarchs begin their return trip, stopping along the way to lay eggs – and die. Their offspring continue the journey, and at last, in late spring or early summer, the descendants of last year's Monarchs arrive in the northernmost part of the species' range. How the original Monarchs know when to leave and where to go, and how their offspring know the return route, are still unanswered questions.

Top to bottom: **Peacock Pansy** *(Precis almana),* **Southeast Asia. Satyrid, Southeast Asia.** *(Cethosia biblis),* **Southeast Asia.**

Red Harlequin *(Laxita damajanti)*, Indonesia. *Right:* Bluebottle *(Graphium sarpedon)*, Malaysia.

Lycaenid, Central Africa. *Below:*
(Axiocerses harpax), Africa.

Other butterflies, including the Red Admiral, American Painted Lady, and Buckeye, extend their ranges northward every summer, breeding in regions where no member of their species spends the winter. But these northern visitors do not travel south when cold weather arrives. Instead they die, to be replaced the following year by another generation of doomed immigrants. A few southern sulphurs and other species travel north in late summer, and can sometimes be seen hurrying southward in the fall, but these immigrants do not breed in the north, and it is doubtful that any of them survive this unexplained journey. None of these visitors is a true migrant like the Monarch, since no round trip is made.

Top to bottom: **Acraeid, East Africa. Nymphalid, Africa.** *Iolaus,* **Africa.**

(Metamorpha elissa), South America.
Below: Cracker Butterfly *(Hamadryas glauconome)*, Central America. *Opposite:*
Owl butterfly *(Caligo)*, South America.

Nymphalid, Central America.

Top to bottom: Daggerwing *(Marpesia iole),* Central America. *Panacea prola,* South America. Daggerwing *(Marpesia corinna),* South America.

A careful observer will be able to see nearly all of the many activities of butterflies. Although collecting butterflies has long been a popular hobby, it is seldom necessary now that so much is known about the butterflies of North America, Europe, and Japan. Watching butterflies, like watching birds, is just as much fun, and doesn't require the killing of these beautiful creatures. All one needs is a keen eye and one of the many excellent field guides.

Opposite: Anartia amathea, South America. Metalmark *(Amarynthis meneria),* South America. *This page: Baeotus japetus,* South America. *Below:* Metalmark *(Caria manitea),* South America. *Overleaf: Haetera piera,* South America.

Episcada mira, South America. *Left:*
Chorinea, South America. *Opposite:*
Nessaea aglaura, Central and South
America.

Collectors, in their determination to add another rare butterfly to their trove, miss many marvelous sights. Identification is now a simple matter, and there is much to see. Anyone who tries the hobby of butterfly watching will soon come across a pair of Red-spotted Purples fluttering in their courtship ritual over a country road, or a female Common Sulphur deftly placing her tiny egg on a clover leaf, or an autumn Monarch flying steadily southward down a busy city street, and will be glad there is no net handy to end such a small but significant drama. The reward will not be a specimen, but the satisfaction of seeing a natural event and understanding what it means.

Top and bottom: **Crimson-patched Longwing** *(Heliconius erato),* **southern Texas to South America.** *Center:* **Zebra Longwing** *(Heliconius charitonius),* **southern United States to South America.** *Opposite, top:* **Temenis laothoe, South America.** *Below:* **Junonia, South America.**

Pierella dracontis, South America. *Below: Pyrrhopyge cometes*, South America. *Opposite and overleaf: Catagramma*, South America.

Index of Photography